AF326604

39
Poems for
Christine

BRAD DREW

39 Poems for Christine

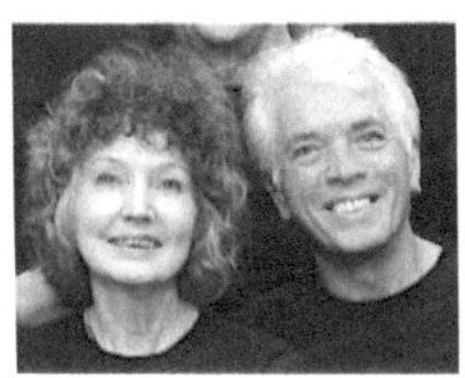

BARDDRIEV PRESS

For D C G

Layout and Book Design: Brad Drew
Drawings and prints by Brad Drew

PROLOGUE

I WAS MARRIED at the tender age of twenty-one: a young age, even back then, at a time when such early embarkments were more common perhaps than they are now. My sisters and most of my contemporaries did just that and probably most survived in some fashion or other. Mine lasted for something less than five years and then, did not.

I was midway through my architecture course at the university when we married, full of hopes and ideals and dreams that this moment would go on like this forever and nothing would ever change ... or so, I thought ... but at a time just short of completing my degree, everything changed while I slept at my desk, preparing my thesis. I slept, not fully-unconscious but in one of those dream states, powerless to change the outcome. And thus, in a few short months, I became an architect and simultaneously, I became a single man once more.

And years passed ... I dabbled in theatre; I travelled to London with a dream of a life in the theatre and instead, found myself working as an architect assisting to build a theatre in the Barbican, for some number of years there before returning to my home town back in Australia, now on its way to fast becoming a city in its own right. Returned there, I continued my life in architecture on home soil and initially, continued to pursue my alter-life as a fine printmaker: a discipline and love acquired during those years in London and taken up in earnest back on home soil, where it ran on for some more years in parallel with my daytime endeavours as a design architect; as had been my main role in London also. And life moved on through its seasons.

* * *

IN THE BEGINNING, there was poetry and the soul of the hopeless (but always hopeful) romantic ... this somewhat unnecessary confession for those who might not have already divined that fact. The poetry had its genesis in a prelude to London – some time post-marital by this stage but in the arms and charms of a romance, well-fitted to inspire its writing: raw as much of it was at that time. It came as an expression, an outlet, for what could not be said in the light of day in any other way but verse. And so, in a sense, it has remained.

I might add that what grew later over succeeding years, as an aim to create poetry, became more consciously deliberate in itself and ever sought refinement; so the scope and realm of focus moved beyond that of simply romantic expression, taking in a wider range of subjects demanding commentary; but as is (or should be) the creation of poetry, it remains an act of seeking to express more than mere complaint or commentary, as might be accomplished in everyday speech or prose.

And so, in London, poetry sought me out again and there, it developed a consciousness of its own and I wrote once more: for yet another moment of an intense but short-lived romance, one destined to quietly persist in the background for many of the succeeding years; this in poetic terms, being interspersed with the occasional moment of everyday observations.

With severance from London and the muse who there sought me out, the poems ceased for a very long period until London's muse, one day long-distant, returned to her and my home town, now a city; there, to pluck me out of my fruitless twenty-year hiatus elsewhere; and in doing so, play her part in awakening the poetic impulse once again. She was not destined to resume her former role (being herself, as I again experienced, of an elusive butterfly nature) but for one important moment, she bore the grail I sought, home to me, rescued me from oblivion descending, and reawakened my sleeping heart.

These intervening decades saw the passage of false starts and pursuits, all in the name of love and romance: the ideal, the personal grail I had kept before me through these many years, responsible for any number of false starts and thus, eventual disappointments. Thanks to the return of my London muse, the poetic consciousness and drive had returned with a strength and purpose, leading me on (I trust) to do better things.

* * *

IN TIME, my home-town, now-city was abandoned in favour of a move to the Blackall Range hinterland of the Sunshine Coast. There, the grail quest continued after a fashion while the poetic

39 POEMS FOR CHRISTINE

impulse continued to gain and diversify with its own strengths; occasionally touching on the quest but concerning itself with an ever widening range of life observations ... and I discovered like-minded poetic friends ... and in time, we collected ourselves together, naming ourselves the Pente Poets.

* * *

THEN, ALONG CAME CHRISTINE: not an overnight event, but a friend who became a love, a companion and a potent muse: a grail reclaimed as life's autumn gained momentum and our respective winters approached.

She was a talented singer of classical training and owned a bookshop: the last of a long succession of such back in Brisbane, before relocating with her sometimes-reprobate Irish husband to manage a new bookshop venture on this same Blackall Range. I befriended Maurice, the husband as he tended their bookshop, charming myself and other locals in the process; and I truly only befriended her, upon joining the same community choir in that local village.

We sang together as members of our little village choir and then one day, Maurie died. For all that he fell short of, and for all of his Gaelic charm, I was moved by his passing. Wishing to pay tribute, I wrote a villanelle to his demise with the intent of beseeching the village populace to not pass him by on the basis of his failings but to see the depths which I had seen.

* * *

39 POEMS FOR CHRISTINE

A FURTHER FOUR YEARS passed along – in choral and bookish friendship with Christine and in time, there came a time when I became aware of feelings which reached deeper than mere friendship with this very musical and equally-literary companion.

There is a romantic tradition amongst Greek populations of coming to the intended's family door and tossing in one's hat. On my grail journey, I had once been a longtime member of such a Greek community; and to which same intent, I appeared one day at the bookshop and in turn, tossed in my hat.

A new muse was born; I had found my grail at last ... and the rest is history.

Brad Drew
April 2022

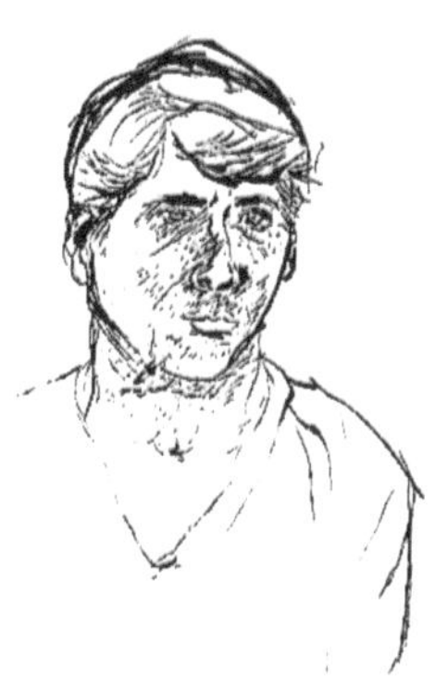

'SELF PORTRAIT'
Quill liner & Indian ink on Fabriano Paper, 1983

CONTENTS

PROLOGUE
THE POEMS:
BLACKALL RANGE
JULY 2006 TO MARCH 2022 :

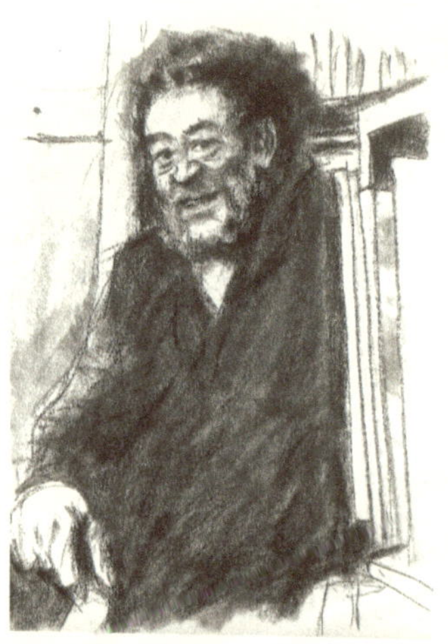

'MAURIE & THE BOOKSHOP'
Conte crayon on Fabriano Paper, 2015

39 POEMS FOR CHRISTINE

FOR MAURIE ... 15 OCTOBER 2006

A gentle soul once gently filled this space,
Was known by all to some or more degree ...
Too late perhaps, we recognise his grace.

Bookshelf to bar and back, each day his pace
Belied the truth that few might truly see ...
A gentle soul once gently filled this space.

Too often kindness has an unseen face,
Consideration looks for no decree ...
Too late perhaps, we recognise his grace.

Though scorned or loved, some truths cannot efface
The truth that lived and loved for all to see ...
A gentle soul once gently filled this space.

So now he's gone and empty seems this place
He occupied so quietly and free ...
Too late perhaps, we recognise his grace.

It's often when one's gone without a trace,
We yearn to know the depths we did not see ...
A gentle soul once gently filled this space;
Too late perhaps, we recognise his grace.

39 POEMS FOR CHRISTINE

SONG FOR A FLAT WORLD

They told me that the world be flat;
that there be dragons
and after them, be monsters.
Venture past a certain point ...
that world will fall away.

Yet, like reborn Columbus
I've set my sails and headed east ...
one compass bearing all I need;
some landfall ... and the promise
of a sought-for new world, calls.

Fair such skies as beckon, lead
into the grail-lit morning ...
and fair the song the trade winds sing
so softly through our rigging;
and fair the course that's set

and fair the seas to follow ...
some landfall on a promised shore
beyond this flat edge world.
Dare to venture past this point ...
all else will fall away.

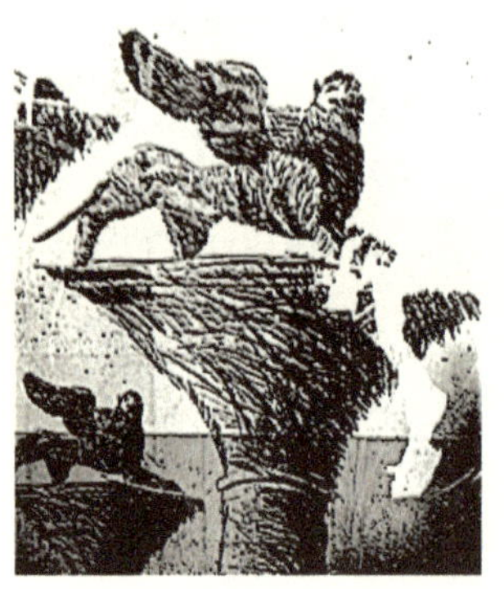

'LIONS OF ST MARKS, VENICE'
Pencil & ink on tracing film, 1983

YET ANOTHER SONG OF SONGS :

'Oh my Beloved, my Song of Songs, and you, the Songstress ...'

CANTO I

Hearken, oh my Love, for I bear no falseness in my words,
    nor with flattery beguile;
    and I know, am well-aware in truth, the timing of our years.
Nor do I speak from kindness, nor in mute consideration –
    this is my Song of Songs
    and is in truth, my sole account of thee ...
Not through rose glasses I, but rather, what my heart knows
    of thee; and what I see, hear, taste, touch, and smell –
    for I am well-pleased, and humbled, and beset by thee.

My Love, you are comely, fair and full with love and joy;
    you are wisdom and mystery to me –
    good sense and soft enigma.
Tender, and terrible of influence, you pervade
    and navigate my sleep;
    drain me of sound reason –
I am lost and helpless before thee
    and I know no more ... no, naught ...
    of life before you entered.

My Love, you are my skin, my joy, my fear
    and daily, the thought of you
    haunts my every moment.
You are my life, my inner substance,
    my suspended sentence
    and my welcome cause.
I could not, would not,
    cage your freedom song
    nor rob thee of its content.

And oh, my Love, my heart delights most
    in your glance
    and your smile lights up my being.
You are my raison d'être; and my heart would ever chase you,
    sans raison ...
    for you are my night and day, my moon and sun,
My every breath of being ... I am eclipsed,
    and I discover
    I am incomplete without thee.

My Love, my Heart, you inhabit my dreams and strew my paths
    with the leaves and litter of longing, while my heart groans
    and breaks, before and on each parting ...
Thus likewise, sighs and leaps my heart upon each meeting
    and I am ever well-favoured;
    and so amply-blessed.
You mark the measures of my sleep and dreams
    and magnify my green and clumsy foolishness;
    in foolishness, I say too much ... too much I fear, of me
    and ask too much of thee.

CANTO II

It is autumn, oh my Love. Our years are numbered –
  the month is April ...
  and July is distant still.
Autumnal bloom enfolds you (as wish I might, would I);
  and you are sweet;
  and filled with sugars of the season.
Your skin is soft and velvet with all fullness
  of the season's bloom, fragrant and enticing;
  and I cherish the linger of its smell, held
  in linen of the bed and bath, you leave behind thee.

Your breath is sweet, your kiss elusive; I pursue them
  both, with ardency and sweet desire ... I chase them
  like some shy doe, for a single moment's touch.
Your touch thrills me and delights;
  gentle and tender;
  your fingers are soft and loving.
You are all gentle shyness of the forest doe, my Love:
  and I would not chase thee down nor cage thee ...
  rather, tend your needs, nourish and protect thee.

Look upon me, oh my Love and smile that I might see
  the loving favour in thine eyes; for thine eyes
  are two soft pools over gentle fervour of thy heart.

Look upon me, oh my Love and smile that I might taste
    the fullness of thy lips; for thy lips are soft,
    generous and breathe the air of love.
Your breath and love are soft and sweet;
    precious as rare oils and spices ... breathe into me
    your essence and the incense of thy love.

Show only to me, your morning and your evening face
    in all purity and freshness ...
    for it is the face I most treasure and adore.
Show only to me, your private face, the first and last
    of each day's wearing ... for it is your most lovely,
    fresh and youthful face
    and wears the cleanness of your love.
I see your morning, evening, private face, oh my Love,
    with all the jealousy of a lover ...
    mine alone to cherish and I would not share its beauty.

Hold me and enfold me, oh my Love –
    store me in your secret places
    and lay me up for winter, should it ever come ...
And I will be warm coals to ease your chill;
    my arm, a safe place and a pillow, for your head;
    my body's curve, thy shelter from the wind.
It is autumn, my Love ... thy season's bloom is greater
    than the months and years that fed it; I would store it
    in the safe place of my heart,
    when winter winds might blow.

CANTO III

I watched for my Beloved, twenty-thousand nights;
    waited on her, called upon her name
    which none did know...
And searched I every lane, outpost
    and byway for her sign.

And lo, I followed to pursue her shadow
    down the byways and backwaters of my life
    to no avail and no effect.
So many times, mistook another for her –
    started at a promise, unfulfilled and incomplete.

I asked in turn, 'Are you she for whom
    my soul does hunger and does yearn...
    are you my heart's great longing and desire?'
And she said, 'Maybe' ... or 'No, but I will stay awhile
    to comfort thee ... but nothing more.'

I thought I saw her once and chased her shadow;
    chased and lost, then chased again ...
    each time the shadow lengthened
And my heart lost heart and closed upon itself
    for still, the name which none did know.

Where are you, my Loved and Longed-for One
    in whom I do believe and trust
    and where do you reside
    these twenty-thousand nights
I've waited for you, called your name,
    the name which none do know?

39 POEMS FOR CHRISTINE

CANTO IV

Hearken, oh my Love, for you are comely
    and more than passing-fair to me; though I know
    full-well the truth in timing of our years.
Oh, you are spring in autumn
    and I would follow thee with faith
    beyond the end of days.
Your eyes are two soft and gentle pools
    where drowns my heart; with cheeks and lips
    lush with bounty of this season's ripeness.

I would taste the fullness of your lips
    and draw into me
    the sweetness of your breath;
For your lips are soft and your speech is sweet.
    Your voice is a balm unto my ears
    and your song, the transport of my heart.
I would hear thy voice
    and hold it to my soul
    when all else fades, is gone.

Speak to me, my Love,
    that I might know your heart
    and hearken to its call.
Speak to me,
    that I might hear your voice
    and mark its music through my soul;
For thy speech is a sweet
    and gentle balm
    which holds me in its thrall.

Behold and listen ...
    the lark who thrills the glade
    fills and binds the soul.
Sing with me, my Love,
    draw near to me
    and sing the balance of our days ...
For you are a lark unto my life,
    evensong and vespers
    for my timely day.

Hearken, oh my Love, for you are comely
    and your voice,
    the joy of lark-song fair to me;
Your eyes, two pools to plunge
    and lips to breathe and taste,
    full transport for my soul;
Your breath as sweet as speech ...
    the spikenard and balm
    to soothe my days.

CANTO V

I glimpsed her, then I found her:
  she whose name none ever knew.
And I drew her to me
  that I might better see her face.
There, loveliness resides and has my heart
  o'ertaken and undone.
And my heart leaps to her, sings in joy
  then cries out in her absence.
Her name is Softness and Beauty
  and I am forever lost.

CANTO VI

Beloved mine, you are all tenderness at once
    and terrible ... all terrible as an army
    that lays siege and sacks my nights;
For sleep as I might, my heart does wake me
    to the drumroll of thy absence
    and my un-slept longing knows no bounds.

Your image, person and your voice
    draw me from sleep and I am beset
    by the banners and the marching of your host.
You walk among my dreams, my Love,
    soft-shod and urgent
    and thy quiet footstep stirs my unquiet night.

Beloved mine, you tend the garden of my being:
    its beds are full to overflowing with the bounty
    of your fruit and blossoms.
You are the bee who tends, for you fertilise
    and feed my hunger; yet steal my appetite –
    shore up my zest for eating.

Come to me, my Love, and lie with me;
    lay off your siege and let your soft-shod footsteps
    pause and rest spoon-wise in mine.
Let the fullness of your autumn fruit
    quench my thirsting mouth
    and quell my always hunger for thee.

Scatter your blossoms on my brow,
    oh sweetest Love, breathe your sleep
    and slumbering heart with mine ...
In the rising and the falling of our breasts
    decamp your army, cease your siege
    and set the standard of your tenderness upon me.

CANTO VII

How beautiful you are, my Love;
    for you are more than passing fair
    and comely in your bearing.
Your very being and your body
    are a well-matched
    and fitting slipper unto mine ...
We do wear each other like fitting and
    well-tailored garments, cut and fashioned
    for all seasons and all weathers.
You are beauty, my Love,
    and you bring me to my knees;
    tear my heart asunder.

Your head is a chalice of goodness
    crowned with wisdom.
Your head is a fine and delicate globe
    wreathed by the wildness of your hair,
    a tangle of sacred and profane delights ...
Your hair is a joy to me
    and your nose is fine and stately;
    in breath, so soft and sweet.
Your cheeks are high and rounded
    set with smiling dimples
    as do ripe pomegranates.

Your eyes are deep with kindness
     and are two pools
     in which I sink, therein to drown.
Your lips are generous
     and I would breathe the honey
     of your lips and tongue.
Your feet are small and eloquent
     and I would kiss and swallow them
     like words of love.
Your calves and thighs are slender saplings
     and your buttocks,
     small and firm as apples.

Your navel is a jewelled thimble
     set in the gentle swell ...
     a small boat moored upon a gentle sea.
The gentle swelling of your belly
     is a soft basket ...
     container of your warmth and goodness.
Your breasts are the bounty of two peaches,
     flowing and full
     with autumn juices ...
And you are full with love for me
     and my pulse quickens
     with your warmth.

Oh, my Love of Loves, you fill me with desire,
    hasten my breath
    for my hand is want upon thee.
Your name is Softness and Beauty,
    Quickness and Desire ...
    and I would fain lie with you
    to be thy grist and core.
Would that I could breathe your breath
    and share the beating of your heart.
    Lock me within thee, oh my Love,
    and never let me go ...
For I am yours alone;
    I am your troth and would
    that thou were truly pleased with me.

CANTO VIII

Hurry, oh my Love, and squeeze out
    the fullness of each moment
For I am your Love and have waited on you,
    called your name,
      these twenty-thousand nights ...
And your name is Lovely, Beauty,
    Softness and Desire,
      and I am full, well-full, of thee.

Your name, which none could name,
    has marked me
      and is a seal upon my heart.
Your flame ignites my veins
    and will not let me rest
      for you are lovely and do blind my sight.
All I am and would be,
    is in thee, my Love
      and you are my purpose and delight.

Come and twine with me, my Love;
    encompass me to hold me close
      and spill the juices of our season ...
For I will drink your heady wine,
    anoint you
      with the nectar of my being;

[33]
And I will cradle thee from the storm,
    my arm a pillow
    and a comfort to thy soul.

Speak to me, my Love, and call my name
    as I've called yours
    and shout, for all the world to hear.
Take my hand and clasp it to your heart,
    pull my arms about you;
    swallow my mouth and drown me in your fire,
For I am mad-crazy for you
    and would have thee melt for me.

Clasp my hand and walk with me, my Love,
    and wear each moment in your breast ...
For I would fain share
    and hold each moment with you –
    adore you to the end.
You are contentment and great joy to me,
    oh my Love ... my reason
    and the absence of all reason.

[With respectful apologies
to one, once Solomon: King.]

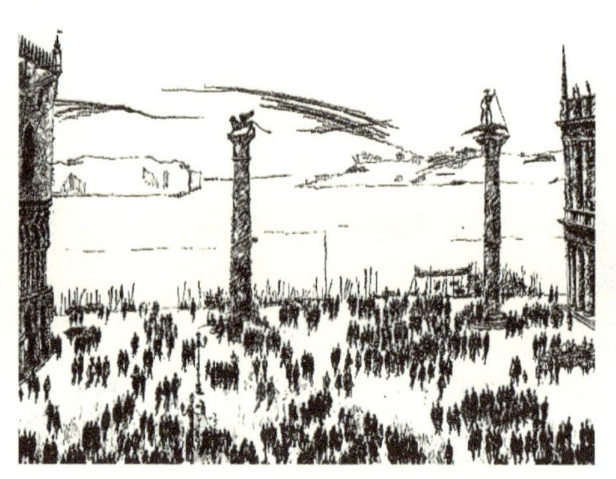

'ST MARK'S SQUARE, VENICE'
Rapidograph pen on Tracing Paper, 1983

YOU ARE MY SONG

You are my evening and my autumn song
and you would be the last I'd wish to sing;
as autumn moves to winter, brief or long –
I'll sing you still, whatever time may bring.
I'll sing your song with passion and with joy,
with tenderness and sweet gentility –
and if time's passage should that voice destroy,
your melody will linger clear and free.

Should you consent to hold me and my love
against your heart and ear for all of time,
your song, your name, will charge my heart above
all others and to yours, my voice will climb.
For you remain my substance, my delight –
you are the song that fills me, day and night.

I THINK YOU HAVE,
MY HEAD UNDONE

I think you have, my head undone;
by all that's light and all that's bright
I know, my heart, you've overrun –

for as your landfall hove in sight
you furled my sails some twelve months past
with all your light, by all that's bright.

Though fly our days and seasons fast,
moored in these new world's waters sound,
you've furled my sails these twelve months past.

Much goodness in your soul resounds
and in your presence, I am blessed –
moored in these waters, safe and sound.

39 POEMS FOR CHRISTINE

I know you have, my heart possessed;
yours is the grail that brings me light
and by your presence I am blessed.

You show me beauty as my right;
I feel you have, my past undone.
Yours is the grail that lights my night –
I know, my heart, you've overrun.

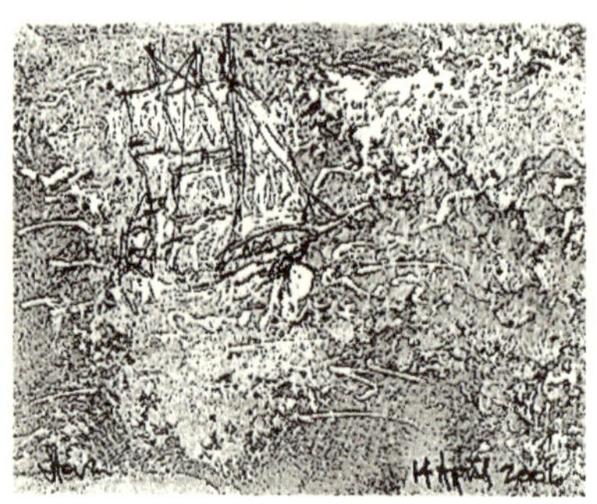

'SHIP IN STORM'
Rollerball pen & whiteout on rusted Arches Paper, 2006

UPON
THE NEW WORLD LANDFALL

A safe and pleasant mooring, sheltered and abundant –
Furled our sails and anchored deep
The sirens' song, lost to their sleep ...
Our ship rides gently on this swell of harboured rest
While all around, our new world's charms attest
The rightness of this landfall.

At harbour's edge, so spreads a landfall verdant ...
This promised shore: this haven, keep;
Both Eden and a place to reap
The harvest of a journey started long years past
When different helmsmen stood before each mast
To hold us each in thrall.

For you alone, are journey's end ...
Your verdant country, I will tend
With love and dedication;
Our damaged paths and fields to mend;
Along your ways I'll gladly wend
With easy step, full-lacking hesitation.

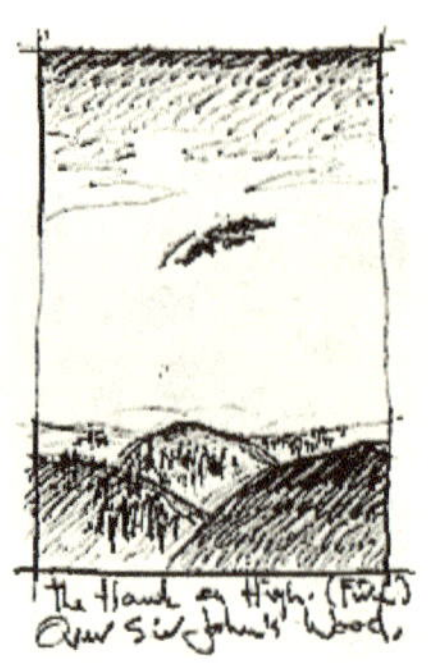

'THE HAWK ON FIRE'
Pencil study for Screen Print, 1980

39 POEMS FOR CHRISTINE

A POEM FOR VALENTINE

The season's February and Cupid's come
in winged haste, all quiver and bow ...
As summer wanes through her last glow.

Hart, hare and hound retreat as kite
soars high, to cry the season's exit –
to enter Autumn and the Fall ...

As once did Psyche's sisters fall
one Eros-lured, in other times
and half a full world distant.

In our own Autumn, Spring revives again –
entreats both wary and the not-so,
to once again be mine and thus to share
the sweetness of this arrow drawn.

39 POEMS FOR CHRISTINE

THREE YEARS OUT

Three years past landfall on this promised shore
when hearts were light and buoyant to the cause
and verdant, through the mists, new Eden rose
around us, fresh with lushness and so pure
the air itself glowed with an inner light ...
So came safe harbour, comfort: sound and bright.

No land is free of goblins, nor of ghosts ...
The same proved true for this new world, our host;
for as we staked our claim, marked out our plots
fey forms were glimpsed to slip past vision's edge –
and as we plumbed and charted out our shore
uncovered shoals and reefs – but little more.

We chart our waters carefully, now we know –
and watch for where waves break amid calm flows;
look out for goblins in the fairy dells
or ghosts whose whispers break the season's spell;
for true our landfall is and fair our barque ...
This journey's ours ... How could we disembark?

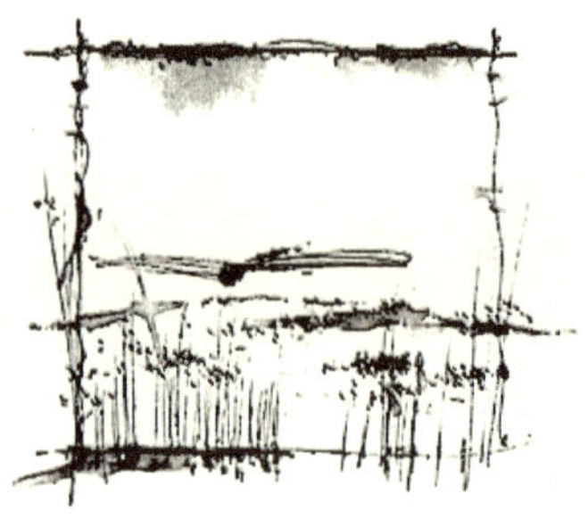

'DRAGONFLY'
Rollerball pen & wash on Arches Paper, 2007

A POEM FOR CHRISTMAS

Morning ... and insistent dawn
slides past shutters, dreams and sleep.
I sense your breathing tuned to mine;
your gentle stirring – and I wonder
if this waking heat is yours
or that of the oncoming day?

Yet one more solstice done –
days shorten on their path to autumn
and beyond ... it's almost Christmas ...
while the gift you are, warms and heartens,
stirs daily – gratitude for your presence
through this Autumn of our seasons.

I watch your waking profile,
then wonder at my own good fortune;
listen for the first birds' calling,
late in this rising heat of day ...
savour this season and our mountain
to thank the world for whom you are.

39 POEMS FOR CHRISTINE

AND OF CONTENTMENT ...

I witness summer's winding down
as February sounds her last retreat
and this year's hares still find delight
in dandelions that grace our hill.

All summer, they have come to meet
and sample full, the weeds that crown
our slopes ... Dawn brings their flight
and dusk returns them still.

No March hare madness this –
save quiet contentment in
familial joys and gentle bliss
as summer greets sweet autumn.

And of contentment, I am mindful
of her easy touch, as all my summers
roll off into one ... The sum and total
of those all, which fell before.

So comes our southern Valentine
lazy with this last of summer's heat –
to quietly beg us all, entreat ...
As I do now ... And ask you to be mine.

39 POEMS FOR CHRISTINE

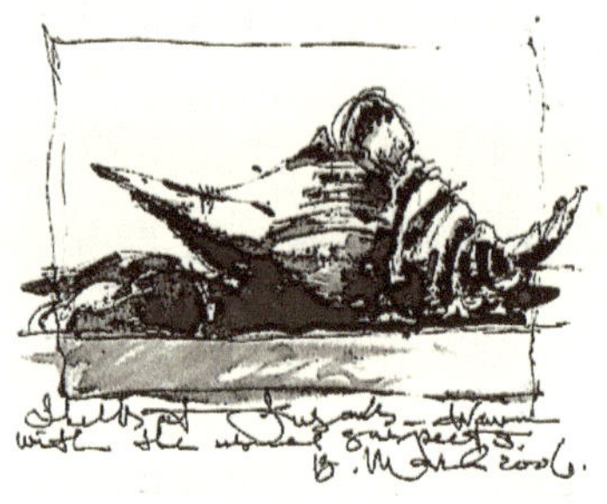

'SHELLS'
Rollerball pen & wash on Arches Paper, 2006

[49]

FOUR YEARS HAVE COME TO US

Four years have come to us and washed these shores
as varied as the tides, which in their surge
bear mostly treasured shells and little more ...

We've seen our journeys into one converge
despite rare storm-front surges from the past
as varied as the tides which by us, surge ...

Our voyage, mostly smooth beneath this mast –
astern, the gentle passage of each now
in spite of storm-front surges from our pasts.

Since setting sail, four years have crossed our bow
to run our length and sparkle in our wake
as churns astern, the passing of each now ...

The purpose of this journey's no mistake;
so we must trim our sails and fair seas urge
to run our length and sparkle in our wake ...

For right a voyage is, that would so merge
while years may come to us and wash our shores ...
then, as we trim our sails and fair seas urge
find mostly pretty shells and little more.

39 POEMS FOR CHRISTINE

SONNET FOR VALENTINE'S

This February has arrived and still
our own fleet hares return to laze and graze
the ever-constant haven of our hill.
Through mists and squall they've come to grace this slope
and brought their young to share these joyous days
which crown their own existence with such hope.

This week has seen them sportive, gay and light;
to leap, spin, turn, cavort across the hill
in mating-mad abandonment's fey flight
to garner all these joys at summer's end;
ward off the threat of hoary winter's chill ...
Such is the essence of the path I'd wend
to tarry with you for this little while
and give you some cause through the mists to smile.

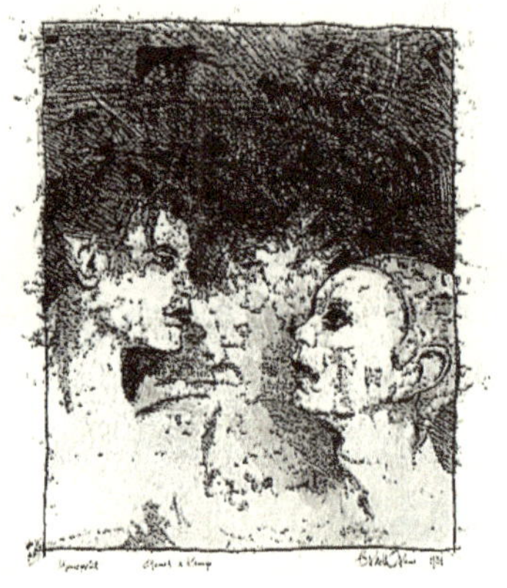

'GENÊT À KEMP'
Mono-print on Japanese Rice Paper, 1981

TO LATER FRIENDSHIPS

Friends come and go throughout the flux of life;
they catch the sun to shine and briefly flare
but often, overtaken in life's shade
they find themselves replaced by other cares ...
These mostly not for reasons false or trite
but simply time and distance lets them fade.
Nostalgia meanwhile, holds them in her arms
to hang around our life like chain-linked charms.

And then, there are those others, coming late:
sparks that smoulder in the embers of our day;
who through their strengths will suffer no such fate;
for you my friend will sidestep all the shade
wherein for time and distance others laid ...
Thus unforgotten, shall you ever stay.

39 POEMS FOR CHRISTINE

A POEM FOR JULY

At this time of year, I find I've now become
aware of odysseys and voyages begun
and sailed through latitudes to longitudes uncharted
as questing eastwards, one reborn Columbus started ...
Sailing far beyond the charted seas he knew
through seasons and through climes of changing hue.

When our new Columbus set out for the edge
of reason, or the world he'd come to know;
or when latter-day Ulysses swore his pledge
to faithfully return at journey's close ...
However might the surge of currents flow,
this was the course he willingly then chose.

Now five years since our odyssey began
and three years since we furled our open sails
to cast our anchor, settle our new land;
surmount with love, what storm-fronts might assail ...
Thus garner in the harvests of our joy
protect our haven and all means deploy
to meld as one, the substance of our lives ...
Plant out our plot so naught but goodness thrives.

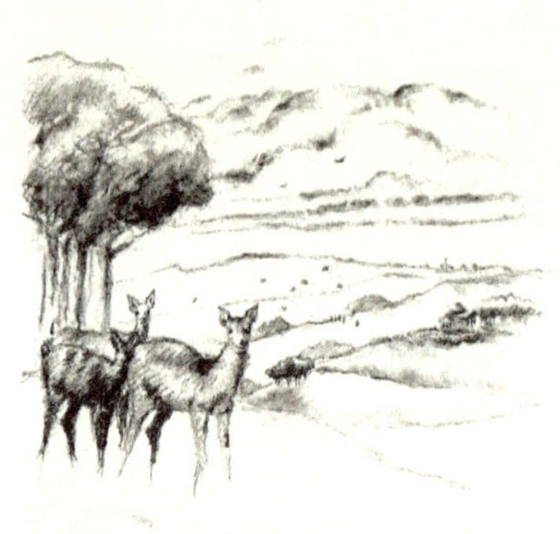

'RICHMOND HILL, 1975'
Notebook Sketch, Graphite Aquarelle & wash, 2020

TWO DAYS OUT FROM VALENTINES

Two days out from Valentine's
and not a poem written
but still, I ask you to be mine;
there's no questioning ... I'm smitten.

39 POEMS FOR CHRISTINE

[57]

This year has come upon us fast.
We never sensed its coming ...
With most things now, not meant to last
we're blessed with love consuming.

As for our hares, they've fled our hill –
moved from our slopes, with February's versing.
I guess they've gone ... At least until
that dog next door stops barking.

We have written of hart, of hares and hounds
and kites in last of summer's flight ...
While hounds cry out, no hares will bound
except through local lanes by night.

While after dusk they may still roam,
their memory will lend us hope
that one day soon, they might come home
again once more, to grace our slopes.

We in the meantime, do our best
to make love count above the rest ...
For I am yours – please you, be mine ...
Make everyday our Valentine's.

39 POEMS FOR CHRISTINE

SO HERE WE ARE ...

So here we are and six years out of port
while your life turns about a new decade ...
Who would have dreamed?
Who would have thought
when we our safe last landfall made,
that freshness at this time of life
could be redeemed?

At water's edge, our settlement abounds
upon a delta merged between paired rivers ...
A flood plain rich in silt
twin years have carried down –
there, flourishes this lushness most diverse.

Our vessel rides now, safely in its harbour
where tides lap gently stem to stern our length
and deep and clean in tidal flow
clear waters wash, to surge about our anchor.
Who could have dreamed? Who could believe
what soundness and what strength
this New World might conceive?

ON DISTANT DOGGY DOTAGE

Viewed up close, each wall becomes a portal
to other worlds: a dim reality, mislaid.
Frozen in time, he becomes the new Zen master
focused on infinity, while paint films melt and fade.

Locked in satori's bright embrace, this empty dog-bowl:
watershed of nothingness, beyond all expectations.
Frozen thus he'll stand, eye to wall at thresholds
of infinity in none-ness ... Never being there at all.

His days turn on this wheel of life, swinging; where
eats and sleep form his meridian; guide his bearings –
always to dream ... And dream, he does ...
There to sit or stand, soft eyelids drooping
and then full-suddenly, to slump ...
Yawn – lick his chops ... Then slump again.

He perambulates with old man gait, oscillating
between arthritic waddle and pure puppy-manic ...
Walking uphill under heavy load, where one shake
will send loose legs all scattering ...
Loose leaves before his Autumn wind,
dispatched to cardinal points in one slipped instant:
old man locomotion and all traction, lost.

Oscillates on sounding of the tea bell ... Reverts
from plodding senior to bright show-pony manic
in one eye's blinking, legs all a-skitter
round about and under a high-borne food bowl ...
There to leap and dance high galliards of joy:
anxiety's relief, when She-who-must-be-loved
returns with bowl, to boon some treat.

And thus-rewarded for his patience,
he'll have the last word with a pee
in unexpected places mostly; and, with stress removed,
drift off to dream enlightenment again.

Perhaps all dotage holds such realms of shadow
lost in light ... Where eyesight blurs;
where hearing fades; and cunning of the old
lights all such hidden places, in a twilight of the senses
not at all what it might seem ...
Where faux farragoes of decrepitude
are bound to triumph every time.

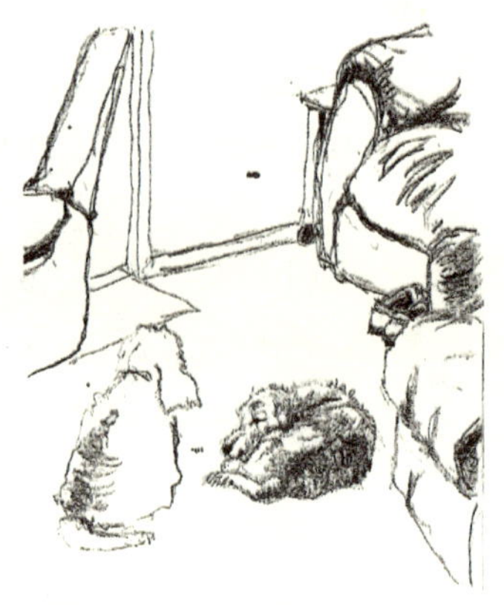

'BENJI DREAMING, HERVEY BAY'
Charcoal pencil on Cartridge Paper, 2015

ONCE MORE COMES CHRISTMAS

Once more comes Christmas
crashing on us in this rush
now come to be expected.
Summer's wings have scarcely spread
when suddenly our longest day is come;
and gone ... A metaphor for life really.

So spread our days to skip before us,
spinning out of sight.

This year has seen our hares move on ...
Our hill un-grazed, to languish in its sea
of unchecked weeds – and weeds, I do not wish for us;
no more than so, might you.
Their pretty golds and mauves, all come and gone!
How fitting for the season: these Father Christmas
seed heads, standing in their stead.

I came here once to love you –
to nurture and support through all our seasons;
cherish you and serve you come what may.
For any weeds which grew, I do regret ...
And with this once-more Christmas time,
I'll clear them from our slopes; refresh this soil.

39 POEMS FOR CHRISTINE

OF LATE, AT NIGHT, OUR LANES

Of late, at night, our lanes themselves are bare
while neighbours' hounds still bark their rowdy way
through life and seasons, quickly, day by day ...
To guarantee the absence of our hares:
once great delights of summer, now dismays.

Another twelve months now have come and passed ...
Once more, our February slides upon us –
bereft of fanfare, leaving us non-plussed.
No more of joyful gambolling hares: they're past;
reminders gone, to which we must adjust.

This year, no hint of summer's winding down:
so hot, the Day of Lovers never felt ...
A Valentine's to make all steam and melt
on even this, our mountaintop of towns
gone quiet in this heat, as forecasts spelt.

In spite of such discomforts, I still hold you dear
and bring you joyful Valentine, with all good cheer.

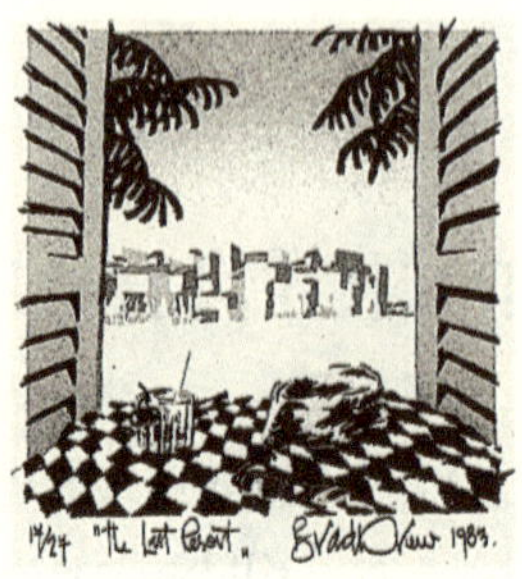

'THE LAST RESORT'
Screenprint on Arches Dessin Paper, 1983
[From the full-colour original]

SEVENTEEN-SEVENTY OBSERVED

With melting-down of day across our bay
the languid air exhales and stills its breath ...
if for an instant. Vain though it might try
to hold day's pulse in check,
an impulse to inhale, at length gives way.

So breathe it does, the very bay to tremor
in this late day's holy, speckled blaze ...
the curtains stir and bougainvillea quiver.

39 POEMS FOR CHRISTINE

Across the bay, the coastal sand-dunes haze,
lost in the build of shimmering sea-alight
where mirrored rippling blinds and sears the eyes
as setting sun sparks water to ignite ...
in brilliance, burning bright enough to daze.

Our atmosphere is charged, light breezes gather ...
tremble ... and on our Naked Bow, all sways
as dusk-bent stirrings herald forth cool weather.

Sun setting on bay's rim, one moment flares ...
igniting far-flung ranges still in reach
while nearer, water with its coastline fades
as mute, the open arms of evening stretch
a fast embrace to hold all in her shades.

Night settles in and then all pales.
The stars and mooring lights switch on.
The bay breathes in – day's light is gone
and all about, our earth exhales.

39 POEMS FOR CHRISTINE

SOME SEVEN YEARS
HAVE PASSED

Some seven years have passed since first we sailed
our craft, to plumb these unknown ocean depths
(Such years, as now, reflect my own decade).
I had thought then, how with that step
to claim some past ports' joys, mislaid
when on horizon's rim, lush lands were hailed.

So hoisting anchor, sail we did
as fast, our New World hove in sight
and to that promised shore were led
our aspirations ... Love come late.

So seven years have passed beneath our bow
while sometimes, beasts rose up from depths far past;
though none of substance dwindled in our wake ...
Our voyage destined, naught might mar
the purpose which these years could yoke
to strengthen our resolve, both then and now.

Our harbour's safe; protected; strong;
sound breakwaters shield our mooring ...
While fo'c'sle bells, these years will ring
out clear, our odyssey's unfolding.

39 POEMS FOR CHRISTINE

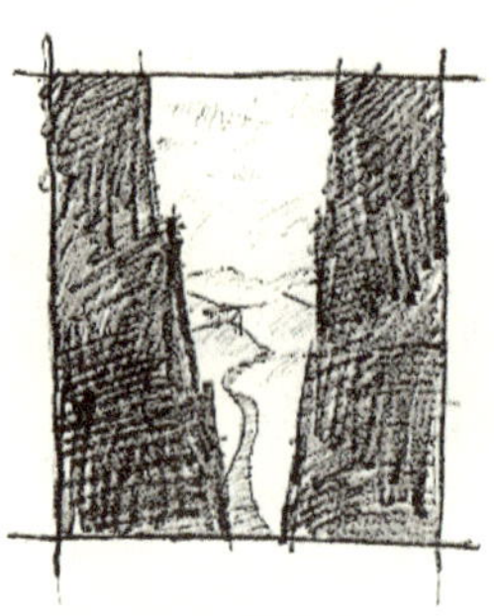

'RAVINE'
Pencil Notebook Study for Screenprint, 1979

39 POEMS FOR CHRISTINE

I WOULD, IF COULD,
SING UNTO YOU ...

I would, if could, sing unto you a season
before the joy of innocence was lost;
before the times of binary-fostered reason
burnt down bridges rationality had crossed.

I'd grant us all a season in much simpler times;
a season long before the web was spun ...
where urgent self-promotion had no walls to climb
when time was leisurely, no race to run.

I'd sing you slow perfection's Christmas tidings;
a carol crafted lovingly with joy;
no settling for the fast-fix now abiding ...
some thoughtful patient savour to employ.

So as we move now through another Season
let's strive for balance in this fledgeling reason.

39 POEMS FOR CHRISTINE

YET ONCE AGAIN A HEAT WAVE

Yet once again a heat wave
to summon up this Day for Lovers ...
Steam our nights and drive our days indoors.

Here, on our gentle Range enclave
bright Mercury now rises up to hover ...
Suck up humidity in temperatures that soar.

These past two years, our hill the hares have fled.
We blame our next-door neighbours' hounds
whose baying chased our hares, now gone instead ...

And still we've missed their daily gambolling flights;
their lazing on our hill; their bounds
seen only now, along its lanes by night.

Small joy! This summer's seen our hares retrace
their steps in boldness; claim our hill
to bless it with their shy and gentle grace ...

One sign that good things never travel far ...
Though maybe hid from sight, they're with us still.
And nor shall time or absence mar
the force which urges us combine
through every day, with Valentine.

39 POEMS FOR CHRISTINE

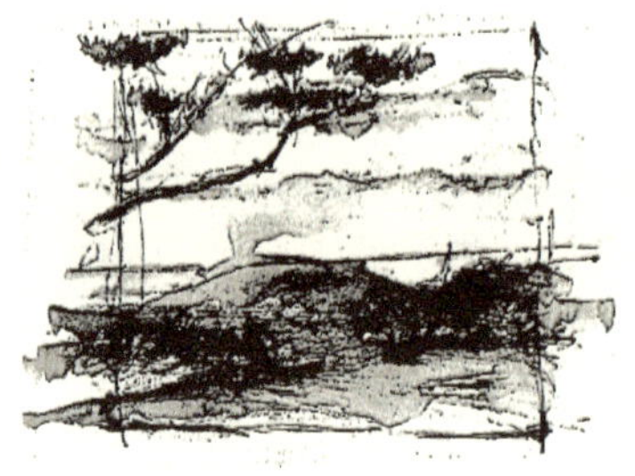

'FROM FALCONCOURT'
Rollerball pen & wash on Arches Paper, 2012

THERE WAS A TIME
THE HEAVENS ...

There was a time the heavens turned and shifted
The stars changed order, constellations moved ...
Across our skies, raised sextants traced their passage.

Through these eight years, the sands of time have sifted
Marked grain by grain our journey as we roved
To set our sails and sights on one last anchorage ...
Safe harbour in a New World glimpsed afar.

The years have flown since that first brave embarkment
With compass set and caution cast to winds
Which carried us and bore us to safe haven

Where storms ebbed in the lee of deep content.
And were there aught our sailor might rescind
He'd answer, 'There is naught that I can fathom
That I'd wish to change or swap for any reason
To set in sight, the wake of your Pole Star.'

39 POEMS FOR CHRISTINE

CHRISTMAS COMES BUT ONCE

Christmas comes but once a year.
Again it's caught me unawares.
I'd thought it safe to say, 'It's near'
then muse ahead, what words to share
but time fooled me – and suddenly it's here!

Yes, suddenly The Day is here.
I'd thought once more, some verse to write
to hail this Season loud and clear
and sing sweet greetings – nothing trite,
to fill your Christmas morn with cheer ...

Yes, fill your Christmas morn with cheer.
Instead, I pour this drivel out
as doggerel, whose form I fear
and scorn in others' word-some bouts
which warrant not the term, 'sincere'.

But Christmas does come once a year
and though our Range dawns bright or drear,
my love for you is always here.
Your presence in my life is dear –
and near to me, my heart you cheer.

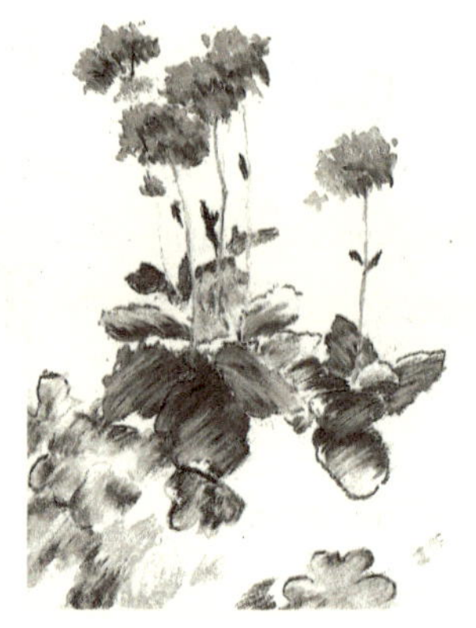

'POTTED PLANT', MT GRAVATT'
Pastel on Cartridge Paper, 1977
[From the full-colour original]

I KNOW THAT SOMEWHERE OUT THERE

I know that somewhere out there, roams our hare.
He's followed us at this time through the years
to mark each exit of our summer's season.
Now Eros draws his bow to loose his flight
tipped with a barb to render sense or reason
mute, nullified; enslaved to all that's fair
and loveliest ... To follow day and night
without one qualm: no doubt; bereft of fears.

The foliage gracing half our slope has flourished.
Dandelions stand their ground on what is left.
Though hid from us, I've marked our hare's swift passage
at odd moments, when he's taken unaware.
Now autumn moves to bear her fruit full-nourished;
Bold Eros girds his bow's enchanted quiver,
with arrows rarely wasted – Aim's so deft.
It's Valentine's ... And once again, his message,
'Might you love me just as much as I love you?'

WE, NESTLED IN SAFE WATERS ...

Settled now – on these calm waters nestled;
our trusted anchors cast into clear depths
to rest here, in this lee of cloud-topped mountains
on this, our ninth year's setting sail;
to venture out upon this voyage,
casting our fates forth on the beckoning sea.

Safe-moored we landed, rising up to settle
on these mist-capped lush and rolling heights
spread out along such fair and verdant ranges;
where under each new season's wind,
we keep our home fires always stoked
to glow and warm the essence of our love.

39 POEMS FOR CHRISTINE

Here spreads and fosters soft companionship
with comforts in our music and with books ...
The arts of all: well-nurtured by the muse
who reigns upon this rampant range
sustaining each soul's nourishment,
so lost within the rush of coastal plains.

Seen far from off these same lush rolling heights,
we might survey the distant sea which brought us
(when clouds and mist rise up to so permit).
Even though most days might ramble
through most-every change of season;
switch clothing up or down at every turn ...

In comfort here, secure on cloud-swept ramparts;
on this eyrie ever safe upon our range;
I know there's nought which I would vary
as we shut and bolt our hatches
battening-down for all which life might throw ...
One time, I set forth like Columbus
to seek out the fabled New World
and found it in the haven of your heart.

39 POEMS FOR CHRISTINE

ONCE MORE, I FIND I'M TAKEN BY SURPRISE

Once more I find I'm taken by surprise
as Christmas rushed up quickly once again.
We'd been so busy watching cloudless skies
I've overlooked the need to prime my pen
whilst wondering if it would rain ... And when?

It will rain sometime – question is, 'Just when?'
This year we need it more than we have most
with weather taking on this nasty spin ...
As fires rage, homes, animals are lost,
while absent politicians juggle costs

With scant regard for common people's costs –
where smoke and mirrors cloud the light of day;
obscure most rights and liberties fast lost ...
And still more droughts and fires, come what may,
while best that they can offer, is to pray.

In spite of dire disasters, I would pray
you health and happiness for all our years –
surmount all obstacles to come our way;
bring light of hope and joy to banish fears
when Christmas chimes ring out so loud and clear.

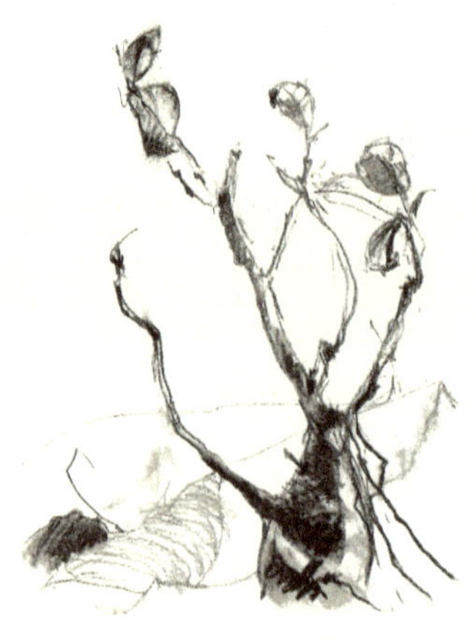

'STRUGGLING POT-PLANT, HERVY BAY'
Notebook sketch with charcoal pencil, 2015

VALENTINE'S 2021

These past twelve months have rushed by, passed us all;
The world we live in, held in mortal thrall ...
But as the season moves once more to Fall
The boy with bowstring answers to its call
And loads his quiver up with arrows sweet
To impale every lover he should meet.

Yet still, our Harry hastens to this hill
To gambol through the weeds and drink his fill
Of dandelions rife where yellows spill –
While giving every heart sweet cause to thrill
And with our coming Valentine's to beat;
To tremble as a breeze through ripened wheat.

So with the advent of this Valentine,
I plea you please, remain this day as mine.

39 POEMS FOR CHRISTINE

TEN ROUNDS OF SEASONS ...

Ten rounds of seasons drift astern; mark out our happy wake.
Their flotsam shows the course we chose to sail
In marking out the passage of this first for us, decade ...

And so the bell rings, rounding on this first bright marker buoy;
Full-sailing on our journey out unto this fresh new world
Where nothing might cause harm or bring dismay ...

Here seasons and the gentle seas have proven kind to us –
Safe harbour is the place we most have known
And as we round about this buoy, our course for harbour's clear:

No matter how the weather might now make its steady way,
Ten years of seasons with you, then ten rounds of seasons more
Will not my ardor quell, nor ever give me cause,
My ever-questing thirst for you to slake.

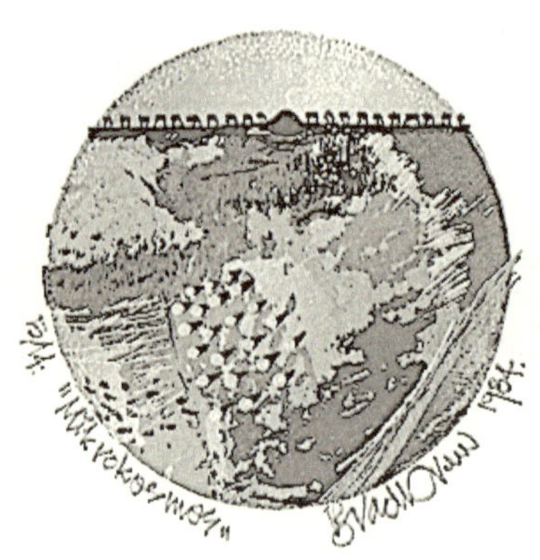

'MICROCOSMOS'
Screenprintprint on Arches Dessin Paper, 1984
[From the full-colour original]

VALENTINES 2022

If our world now seems bereft of rhyme or reason
while countless voices clamour to be heard
and rationale's a concept out of season
prompting chaos and division with their words,
led by experts true or false – who is to say?

If I should stand here, quiet on the sidelines;
withhold from passing judgments, come what may;
refuse to join the babble of so many minds
at odds with one another to belay
the cost and loss to social parity and trust ...

Cast off all fears obsessing for a little while
while Valentine returns, as each year, must ...
Receive his arrows loving and take cause to smile
to gather in my loving, lust and trust –
for it comes thus evermore, sans rhyme or reason.
You remain forever for me, in full season.

39 POEMS FOR CHRISTINE

TWELVE YEARS ...

Twelve years! A dozen; lapsed and fled our scene ...
While all their days (to borrow from Bukowski),
have run away, like wild horses over the hills.
And it seems there was a time when we were keen,
were sharp enough to handle all those spills
and falls which ever seemed at best, unlikely.

For it started when a new Columbus sailed,
undaunted by the concept of flat worlds
where dragons and most other monsters met ...
To regions where his waiting life-quest hailed.
Then, with these bearings, his grail compass set,
all misgivings in the face of gods were hurled.

Safe landfall rose from lifting mists that morning,
as anchors of two lifetimes were outcast
to lodge behind a newfound bay's last shoals.
Completion found relief in that dawn's moorings
when faith lay lightly on this fresh world's goals
and disappointments vanished from lives past ...

39 POEMS FOR CHRISTINE

Twelve years, safe-berthed upon these mountain moorings,
free of flotsam from the past and all it held;
the years and days swift fly away before us
and merge together in each new day's dawning,
heard gently in our butcherbirds' sweet chorus ...
So, the final anthem of our lives might meld
to bring together two small lives compounded
before their final, chaptered lives have foundered.

A GRAIL QUEST REALISED

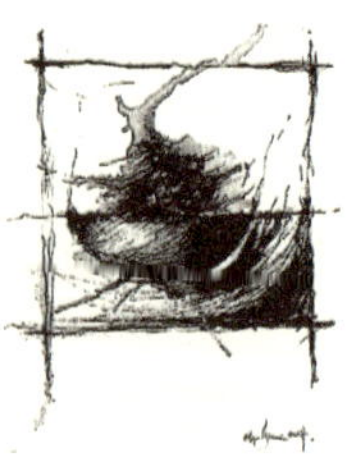

39 POEMS FOR CHRISTINE

39 POEMS FOR CHRISTINE

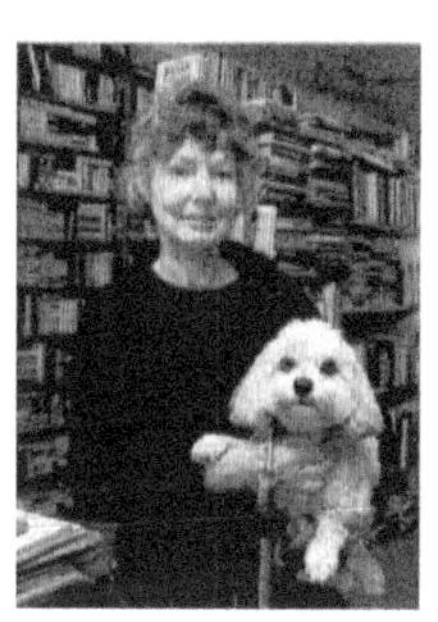

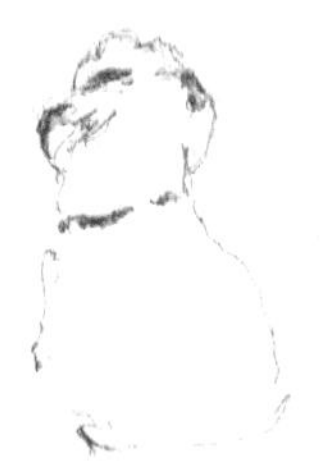